First World War
and Army of Occupation
War Diary
France, Belgium and Germany

58 DIVISION
Divisional Troops
Divisional Signal Company
1 September 1915 - 29 February 1916

WO95/2996/7

The Naval & Military Press Ltd
www.nmarchive.com
Published in association with The National Archives

Published by

The Naval & Military Press Ltd

Unit 10 Ridgewood Industrial Park,

Uckfield, East Sussex,

TN22 5QE England

Tel: +44 (0) 1825 749494

www.naval-military-press.com

www.nmarchive.com

This diary has been reprinted in facsimile from the original. Any imperfections are inevitably reproduced and the quality may fall short of modern type and cartographic standards.

© **Crown Copyright**
Images reproduced by permission of The National Archives, London, England, 2015.

Contents

Document type	Place/Title	Date From	Date To
Heading	58th Division 58th Divl Signal Coy R.E. 1915 Aug-1916 Feb And 1917 Jan-1919 Jun		
Heading	WO95/2996/7		
Miscellaneous	Monthly Statement	03/09/1915	03/09/1915
Miscellaneous	Intelligence Summary & Monthly Statement	03/09/1915	03/09/1915
War Diary	Walton	01/09/1915	04/09/1915
War Diary	Walton To Warren Heath	05/09/1915	05/09/1915
War Diary	Warren Heath	08/09/1915	12/09/1915
War Diary	Little Bealings Martlesham Woodbridge	13/09/1915	13/09/1915
War Diary	Martlesham	14/09/1915	14/09/1915
War Diary	Little Bealings Martlesham Woodbridge	17/09/1915	17/09/1915
War Diary	Warren Heath	18/09/1915	27/09/1915
War Diary	Warren Heath to Washbrook Lines Farm	27/09/1915	27/09/1915
War Diary	Warren Heath	30/09/1915	30/09/1915
War Diary	Washbrook	01/10/1915	01/10/1915
War Diary	Warren Heath	02/10/1915	29/10/1915
War Diary	Warren Heath Ipswich	01/11/1915	31/01/1916
Heading	War Diary Of O.C 58th Divisional Signal Company R.E From February 1st 1916 To February 29th 1916		
War Diary	Bulford	01/02/1916	22/02/1916
War Diary	Ipswich	23/02/1916	28/02/1916
War Diary	Stotfold	29/02/1916	29/02/1916

58TH DIVISION

58TH DIVL SIGNAL COY R.E.
~~JAN 1917 - JUN 1919~~

1915 AUG — 1916 FEB
AND
1917 JAN — 1919 JUN

WO 95/2996/7

Monthly Statement
August. 1 — 31.

58th (London) Divisional Signal Co

A.B.C.

Training.

The Company are carrying out 4 & 5 days schemes, every alternate week. This is being done to train all ranks in the continuous working of Divisional, Brigade & Battallion Signal Offices.

Lines are being laid & reeled up at night. A number of them being laddered.

A signalling school for Infantry Officers, N.C.O's & men, in the Division, has been in progress. A class for Artillery Officers in Buzzer practice has been held daily, & each Battery of Artillery (in turn) have had 10 men weekly undergoing cable laying.

Brigade sections have been working with their respective Brigades & all the signallers of the 173rd Brigade have been working in conjunction with the Signal Company. (by Battallions.)

K2462

3.9.15.

Gordon Kennard.
Major RE(T)
O.C. Signals
58th London Division.

Intelligence Summary
& monthly statement.

[Stamp: 58th (LONDON) DIVISION — 3 SEP. 1915 — GENERAL STAFF]

58th London Divisional Signal Co RE (TF)

Mobilization centre London.

Stations since mobilization. London.
Maresfield
Crowborough
Ipswich
Warren HEATH.

Now stationed at WARREN HEATH.

Date. 3 : 9 : 15.

Gordon Kennard
Major R E (T)
O. C. Signals.
58th (London) Division

K2462.

Army Form C. 2118.

WAR DIARY
or
INTELLIGENCE SUMMARY

58th DIVISIONAL SIGNAL COMPANY.

(Erase heading not required.)

Instructions regarding War Diaries and Intelligence Summaries are contained in F. S. Regs, Part II. and the Staff Manual respectively. Title pages will be prepared in manuscript.

Hour, Date, Place	Summary of Events and Information	Remarks and references to Appendices
WALTON Sept 1st 6.15 P.M. WEDNESDAY.	Termination of 3 days Communication scheme Divisional Signal Co. & Signalling school of Instruction concentrated at WALTON HALL NR. FELIXSTOW. Clarification Test of School commenced	GK
WALTON TO WARREN HEATH. SUNDAY. Sept 5th 2.15 P.M.	Company & Signalling School Return to WARREN HEATH by route march.	GK
WARREN HEATH. Sept 8th Wednesday.	Company on Communication scheme in conjunction with Divisional Artillery. Zeppelin alarm given at 8 P.M. C.E. Returned to quarters 10.45 P.M. nothing seen or heard.	GK GK
WARREN HEATH Sept 11th Saturday.	An Aerial raid warning received at 10 A.M. Nothing seen or heard C.o returned to quarters 11.15 A.M.	GK

Gordon Kinnaird
Major RE

Army Form C. 2118.

WAR DIARY
or
INTELLIGENCE SUMMARY 58th DIVISIONAL SIGNAL COMPANY.
(Erase heading not required.)

Instructions regarding War Diaries and Intelligence Summaries are contained in F.S. Regs, Part II. and the Staff Manual respectively. Title pages will be prepared in manuscript.

Hour, Date, Place	Summary of Events and Information	Remarks and references to Appendices
WARREN HEATH. Sunday Sept 12th 9 A.M.	All horses and mules inspected by Inspector of Remounts from War Office.	GK
LITTLE BEALINGS MARTLESHAM WOODBRIDGE Monday Sept 13 1. PM	The Divisional Signal Cos left WARREN HEATH for a six day continuous Communication scheme to practice Intercommunications in a Division with daily advances. The scheme was carried out in conjunction with all the Battalion signallers of 175/3DE, a fitted in on the Tuesday with the Divisional Artillery scheme	GK GK
Martlesham Tuesday Sept 14th 11. P.M.	Zeppelin passed overhead dropping explosives which fell approximately one mile from martlesham HALL. No damage done. Bombs were dropped in a great hurry due to the fact that Anti-aircraft gun opened fire on her.	GK

Gordon Kenney
Major RE

Army Form C. 2118.

WAR DIARY
or
INTELLIGENCE SUMMARY

58th DIVISIONAL SIGNAL COMPANY.

(Erase heading not required.)

Instructions regarding War Diaries and Intelligence Summaries are contained in F. S. Regs., Part II. and the Staff Manual respectively. Title pages will be prepared in manuscript.

Hour, Date, Place	Summary of Events and Information	Remarks and references to Appendices
LITTLE BEALINGS MARTLESHAM WOODBRIDGE FRIDAY 17th/9/15	Last day of scheme. G.O.C. inspected Companies Automents at WARREN HEATH during absence.	GK
		GK
WARREN HEATH Saturday 18th/9	Divisional Signal Co. returned by route march to Warren Heath	GK
WARREN HEATH 8 P.M.	Stand-By order received from 9HQ all Technical equipment. Blankets, Food & Forage for two days packed. and Company ready to move.	GK
Sunday 19th/9 WARREN HEATH 3·30 PM	Period of vigilance declared closed	GK

Gordon Kennard
Major RE
O C 58th Divisional Signal Coy

Army Form C. 2118.

WAR DIARY
or
INTELLIGENCE SUMMARY

58th DIVISIONAL SIGNAL COMPANY,

(Erase heading not required.)

Hour, Date, Place	Summary of Events and Information	Remarks and references to Appendices
WARREN HEATH Saturday Sept 25th 5.P.M.	Supper & Concert held the Company & representatives from each of the Battalion Signalling Sections with their Batt. Sig. Officer attended anniversary of formation of 58th Divisional Signals.	GK

WARREN HEATH
Sunday Sept 27th
3.PM
	4th DIVISIONAL SIGNALLING SCHOOL OF INSTRUCTION Commences for ONE MONTHS duration
	Following number reported
	Infantry 48
	Artillery. 40
	Officers undergoing instruction 4
	R.E. 2
	                 ——
	TOTAL 94.
	Divisional Sig Instructors 9
	Sig Officer in charge 1
	                              ——
	                              104.
		Specially arranged with O.C. Troops Warren HEATH as the 2 Line units having just come in & have had no instruction yet for their battery signallers
		
		GK
		
		Gordon Kennard
		Major R.E.
		O.C. Sig Reserves
		58

1247 W 3299 200,000 (E) 8/14 J.B.C. & A. Forms/C. 2118/11.

Army Form C. 2118.

WAR DIARY
or
INTELLIGENCE SUMMARY

58th DIVISIONAL SIGNAL COMPANY.

(Erase heading not required.)

Instructions regarding War Diaries and Intelligence Summaries are contained in F. S. Regs., Part II. and the Staff Manual respectively. Title pages will be prepared in manuscript.

Hour, Date, Place	Summary of Events and Information	Remarks and references to Appendices
Warren Heath to Washbrook Lines Farm. Monday Sept 29th	4 Cable detachments of Company leave by Route march for Washbrook for 7 days Night Cable work. Laying & Poling of Lines.	GK
Warren Heath Thursday Sept 30th	Case of Scarlet Fever reported by M.O among one of the remaining men at Warren Heath. Hut isolated, all occupants of Hut isolated. Another suspected case reported. Permission obtained from D.H.Q for cable detachments to remain at Washbrook & await developments at Warren Heath.	GK GK GK

Gordon Kennard
Major RE
OC Signals
58th Division

Army Form C. 2118.

WAR DIARY
or
INTELLIGENCE SUMMARY
(Erase heading not required.)

58th Divisional Signal Co R.E.

[Stamp: 58th LONDON DIVISION GENERAL STAFF 3-NOV.1915]

Instructions regarding War Diaries and Intelligence Summaries are contained in F.S. Regs., Part II. and the Staff Manual respectively. Title pages will be prepared in manuscript.

Hour, Date, Place	Summary of Events and Information	Remarks and references to Appendices
Friday, Oct. 1. WASHBROOK	Signal Co. at Washbrook. Laying lines at night.	G.K.
Sat. Oct 2. Warren Heath	16 men returned from leave & 18 horses sent to join Company at WASHBROOK.	G.K.
Oct 6th Warren Heath	Company paraded for Munition Investigation. 12 men volunteered.	G.K.
Oct 7th -	20 men from No 4 Section who were isolated through the outbreak of Scarlet Fever, were sent to the Infirmary to have clothes disinfected.	G.K.
Oct 8th -	Company returned from Washbrook. 20 men isolated proceeded home on leave.	G.K.
Oct 11th -	16 men from Artillery units commenced 14 days course in Cable Laying & Telephones with this unit.	G.K.
Oct 13th - WARREN HEATH	Zeppelin warning received from East Coast. Company & Fire Picquet turned out. Horses previously arranged. Zeppelins (two) heard overhead 11.15 p.m. Travelling N.E. at a very great height, not to be seen. Firing heard & Bombs dropped. No local damage. Result of firing unknown.	G.K.
Oct 15. WARREN HEATH	Warning received at 11.15 p.m. that raid (airship) was expected. Usual precautions taken, nothing seen or heard.	G.K.
Oct 18th -	Inspection of Horses by A.D.V.S.	G.K.
Oct 21st -	Company took part in Field operation with the 58th Division	G.K.
Oct 23rd -	98 Signallers of the Division returned to their units after undergoing one months Course of instruction with the Company most of them qualified as efficient signallers.	G.K.

Army Form C. 2118.

WAR DIARY
or
INTELLIGENCE SUMMARY
(Erase heading not required.)

58th DIVISIONAL SIGNAL Co RE.

Hour, Date, Place	Summary of Events and Information	Remarks and references to Appendices
Oct 25th Warren Heath	The Signallers of the 6th Battalion Lts of London Rgt. 174 BDE paraded with the Company to undergo their Classification Test.	Q K.
Oct 26th Warren Heath	As above.	Q K.
Oct 27th Warren Heath	The Signallers of the 7th Battalion 174 BDE paraded with the Company to undergo their Classification tests.	Q K.
Oct 27th 9.30 P.M.	Warning received as to air raid. Nothing seen or heard.	Q K.
Oct 28th Warren -	Classification tests of 7th Bat. continued	Q K.
Oct 29th - -	Company took part with the 58th Division in Field Operations	Q K.

Gordon Hammond
major
O.C. 58th Divisional Signals
5th Nov 1916

Army Form C. 2118.

WAR DIARY
or
INTELLIGENCE SUMMARY
(Erase heading not required.)

58th (London) Division Signal Co.

Instructions regarding War Diaries and Intelligence Summaries are contained in F. S. Regs., Part II. and the Staff Manual respectively. Title pages will be prepared in manuscript.

Hour, Date, Place	Summary of Events and Information	Remarks and references to Appendices
Warren Heath. Special.		
November 1st/15	The Signallers of 8th Battn reported for Classification test.	
7	Col Shell visited Camp.	
9	Tactical Exercise written for Staff.	
11	Tactical Exercise (night) both with of Division wrote for Staff.	
15	Signalling Officer for Artillery (Command).	
19	Divisional Hospital Rising Scheme wrote for Staff.	
24	All Horses & Mules Reviewed & Inspected by Col Long.	
26	Tactical Exercise with write-up Division wrote for Staff.	
27	Divisional Hospital Rising Scheme wrote for Staff.	
30	Major Jordan O.C. 1st Army Signal Co. visited the unit.	

A. R. Burt
for O/C 58th Division Signal Co.

Army Form C. 2118.

WAR DIARY
or
INTELLIGENCE SUMMARY
(Erase heading not required.)

Hour, Date, Place	Summary of Events and Information	Remarks and references to Appendices
Dec 9th 1915	Company in Divisional scheme with rest of the troops at MARTLESHAM	OK
13th 1915	Signal Coy carried out a commemoration scheme without troops in the vicinity of BUCKLESHAM.	OK
26th 1915	Christmas greetings from the King read to Company	OK
28th 1915	Inspection by G.O.C. on Martlesham Heath	OK
30th 1915	A.A.Q.M.G. visited Company	OK

A.T. 3198.

Gordon Kennard
Major R.E.
O.C. Signals
58th Division

Stamp: 58th (LONDON) DIVISION * GENERAL STAFF * 5 - JAN. 1916

WAR DIARY — 58th (Lon) Div. Sig. Coy.

INTELLIGENCE SUMMARY

Army Form C. 2118

(Erase heading not required.)

Place	Date	Hour	Summary of Events and Information	Remarks and references to Appendices
Warnimont Ecurie	29/1/16		58th Division Signal Company R.E. Company proceeded to Beauval for Special Course.	App.
	3/1/16		Company Returned from Beauval.	App.

58th (LONDON) DIVISION
3 = FEB. 1916

Vincent T.
for O.C. 58th Div. Signal Coy. R.E.

Confidential.

War Diary of

O.C. 58th Divisional Signal Company R.E.

from February 1st 1916 to February 29th 1916.

— War Diary —

Summary of Events and Information.

Hour Date & Place		Remarks and Reference to Appendices
1/2/16 Bulford	Received orders from O.C. 3/1st Wessex R.E. to re-form 2nd line Unit at once preparatory to joining 58th (London) Division. 2nd Lieut. H.P. ROWE recalling him from leave.	
" 2.0 pm	LIEUT. H.P. ROWE reports from leave.	
3/2/16 Bulford	Forwarded nominal rolls of new 2nd and 3rd line Units to O.C. 3/1st Wessex R.E. LIEUT. ROWE recommended as O.C. 3/1st Wessex Signal Coy R.E.	
5/2/16 Bulford	3rd line Unit re-formed and placed on own ration form this day inclusive. 3 R.II. transferred to 3rd line and forged by their Unit.	
9/2/16 BULFORD	2/LIEUTS W.H. JAMES and E.F. RENDELL, 2gre Electrical Engrs, attached to 2/1st Wessex Signal Coy R.E., return to HASLAR BARRACKS, GOSPORT for duty with their own Unit under authority from H.Q. Southern Command.	
— do —	Received orders by wire from H.Q. Southern Command for detachment of 1 Officer and 25 other ranks to proceed to BANBURY on 11th inst. to erect Light power aerial electric lighting cable for munition factory. Train arrangements to be made in conjunction with R.T.O. AMESBURY	
11/2/16 BULFORD 8.45am	Detachment of 2/LIEUT. D.C. HENRY and 24 other ranks left BULFORD for BANBURY	

2//

12/2/16 BULFORD. 1 pm	CAPT. W.C. MICHELMORE granted leave of absence under authority of O.C. 3/1st A.S.S.C. R.E. until midnight Wednesday 15th inst.	
13/2/16 BULFORD. 9 pm	2/LIEUT G.D. ARDEN reports for duty on completion of three weeks Rifle Course at HAYLING ISLAND.	
14/2/16 BULFORD	One R.T.II store in fund returned to D.A.D.R. No 2 CIRCLE S.C. One R.II drawn from app. 60 Remount Depot BULFORD, to replace.	
15/2/16 BULFORD. 9 am	No: H Rifle Range BULFORD allotted to Unit for mornings of Tuesday, Wednesday and Thursday 15th to 17th insts. inclusive.	
16/2/16 BULFORD	Orders received by wire from O.C. 3/1st Wessex R.E. to send advance party to IPSWICH of one Officer and two N.C.Os on the 17th inst.	
17/2/16 BULFORD	3/1st Wessex signal Coy R.E. leave BULFORD for SOUTHBOURNE	
18/2/16 BULFORD 9 am	app. A. Rifle Range BULFORD allotted to Unit for Skill-at-Arms practice.	
19/2/16 BULFORD. 8.45 am	LIEUT. F.G. BRYANT and 2 N.C.Ds. left BULFORD for IPSWICH as advance party.	
20/2/16 BULFORD 9am	Received under Local cover from H.Q. London Command Rise Table of stores for move of 3/1st Wessex Field Coy, 2/3rd Wessex Field Coy and 3/1st Wessex Engine Coy, to NEEDHAM-MARKET and IPSWICH respectively. Acknowledged receipt of same.	
22/2/16 BULFORD 3.30 pm	Unit leaves AMESBURY STATION in one train for IPSWICH.	

3

22/2/16	BULFORD. 9.0 pm	Watered horses at ROMFORD.
23/2/16	IPSWICH 1.20 am	Arrived at IPSWICH. Roads impassable owing to snow and ice.
	7.50 am	Column leaves IPSWICH Station
	9.0 am	Company arrives at WARREN HEATH CAMP, and takes over alloted quarters in huts. Rationed and forged by A.S.C.
	2 p.m.	Reported in person to A/Q 58th (London) Division
24/2/16	IPSWICH 6.30 pm	Received orders from H.Q. 58th (LONDON) DIVISION to proceed with Unit to BALDOCK on Monday the 28th inst. Forwarded train requirements by D.R. to H.Q.
25/2/16	IPSWICH 9.15 am	Received orders from H.Q. 58th DIV. to send advance party of one Officer and six other ranks to BALDOCK the same day.
"	3.0 pm.	2/LIEUT G.D. ARDEN and six other ranks left IPSWICH for BALDOCK with orders to report on arrival to O.C. Depot BALDOCK
25/2/16	IPSWICH	Received notification from H.Q. 58th DIV. that Unit would be inspected at 12 noon on the 26th inst. by A.A. & Q.M.G. 58th DIV.
25/2/16	IPSWICH 9.15 pm	Received wire No RT.3130. from CENTRAFORCE LONDON giving full details for move of Unit to BALDOCK on the 28th inst.
26/2/16	IPSWICH 11 am	Confirmation of above wire received from H.Q. 58th DIV.
- do -	12 noon	All men regimentally employed and nominal rolls of men rejoined from B.E.F. inspected by A.A. & QMG 58th DIV.

4.

26/2/16	IPSWICH. 2.10 pm	Received wire from O.C. Advance Party STOTFOLD giving details of billets etc. for Company in neighbourhood of BALDOCK.
27/2/16	IPSWICH 10 am	Inspection of all horses by V.O. I/c WARREN HEATH CAMP.
28/2/16	IPSWICH. 10.30 am	Half Company leaves IPSWICH Station for HITCHIN arriving at 1.30 pm and marching to STOTFOLD
	12.30 pm	Remainder of Company leaves IPSWICH Station, arriving HITCHIN at 3.56 pm and marching to STOTFOLD, ASHWELL and HINXWORTH

Company quartered in billets with subsistence as under —

        H.Q. and No 1 Section   STOTFOLD
        No. 2 Section   ASHWELL
        No. 4 Section   HINXWORTH

Horses stabled in open stables and forage by HITCHIN Supply Depot.

C.Q.M.S. and four other ranks remain at WARREN HEATH CAMP. IPSWICH in charge of 3 sick horses.

2/LIEUT. BRYANT remains at WARREN HEATH sick, unable to travel.

29/2/16	STOTFOLD 11.15 am	Unit inspected by COMMANDANT Signal Service Training Centre
	1.30 pm	Bath detachments by double lorries to ASHWELL and HINXWORTH

                                                 N.E. Nicholson
                                                 Capt. RE.T.F.
                                       O.C. 5ZZ Div Signal Coy RE(T)

www.ingramcontent.com/pod-product-compliance
Lightning Source LLC
Chambersburg PA
CBHW081509160426
43193CB00014B/2633